Boat Trip Down the Dart

Totnes to Dartmouth

Bob Mann

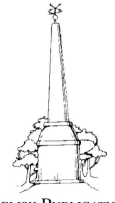

OBELISK PUBLICATIONS

OTHER OBELISK PUBLICATIONS INCLUDE:
Around & About the Haldon Hills, Chips Barber
The Lost City of Exeter, Chips Barber
Diary of a Dartmoor Walker, Chips Barber
Adventure Through Red Devon, Raymond B. Cattell
Under Sail Through South Devon & Dartmoor, R. B. Cattell
Diary of a Devonshire Walker, Chips Barber
The Great Little Dartmoor Book, Chips Barber
The Great Little Exeter Book, Chips Barber
Made in Devon, Chips Barber & David FitzGerald
Dartmoor in Colour, Chips Barber
Burgh Island & Bigbury Bay, Chips Barber and Judy Chard
Dark & Dastardly Dartmoor, Sally and Chips Barber
Tales of the Unexplained in Devon, Judy Chard
Exeter in Colour and *Torbay in Colour*, Chips Barber
Haunted Happenings in Devon, Judy Chard
The Totnes Collection, Bill Bennett
Walking "With a Tired Terrier" In and Around Torbay, Brian Carter
The Ghosts of Exeter, Sally and Chips Barber
The Ghosts of Torbay, Deryck Seymour
The Ghosts of Berry Pomeroy Castle, Deryck Seymour
The Great Little Totnes Book, Chips Barber with Bill Bennett
Tales of the Teign, Chips Barber and Judy Chard
Ten Family Walks on Dartmoor, Sally and Chips Barber
The A to Z of Dartmoor Tors, Terry Bound
The Ghosts of Brixham, Graham Wyley
The Great Little Plymouth Book, Chips Barber
Plymouth in Colour, Chips Barber
Weird and Wonderful Dartmoor, Sally and Chips Barber

For further details of any of our titles, please contact us at the address below or telephone Exeter (0392) 68556

Acknowledgements: Many thanks to all those who have, conspicuously or inconspicuously, helped with the creation of this book, especially: Chips Barber, James Bellchambers, Bill Bennett MBE, Dick Causton, the Devon members of NSUK, David Neil, The Oilstones, Robert Reeves, Mrs V. Rehberg, Sam Richards, Charles Riggs, Karen Thomas, Stephen Westcott and Helen White. *This book is dedicated to Maya.*
Plate Acknowledgements: Front/Back Cover by Chips Barber; Sketch Map on Inside Front Cover by Sally Barber; Various old views provided by Bob Mann and Chips Barber apart from Page 27 (Peter Tully); All other photos by C Barber apart from Page 26 (B Mann).

First published in 1991 by
Obelisk Publications, 2 Church Hill, Pinhoe, Exeter, Devon
Designed by Chips and Sally Barber
Typeset by Sally Barber
Printed in Great Britain by Penwell Ltd, Kelly Bray, Callington, Cornwall

Boat Trip Down the Dart
Totnes to Dartmouth

It is a well-established conceit for a Devon-born writer to begin by explaining that, having had the good fortune to have come from so perfect a place, it is very difficult for him or her to do justice to anywhere else, which must, inevitably, suffer in comparison. I must confess to feeling this way about Totnes and the River Dart, imposing them as a standard on all other towns and rivers which, of course, none can ever come up to, despite their undoubted merits.

There is something so pleasing and archetypal about the setting and relationship of river and town: the Dart flowing from high moorland to the sea, the steep old market town on its bank, secure and contented amidst rich farmland like a miniature city-state, still ending neatly at the beginning of the countryside (at least in most directions); then the dark brown waters of the estuary winding between high, tree-covered hills to finally join the sea between two castles. But it is not necessary to have been born here to feel this deep mythic quality about the lower Dart and its landscapes. It is this that people respond to and which draws them back year after year and makes them never want to leave, whether they come simply for tranquillity and relaxation or, as increasing numbers do, in order to be creative, for healing and transformation or to live in a more natural and authentic way than can be done in other parts of the country. The Dart, though so beautifully and supremely itself, represents all rivers; Totnes has an ambience all its own yet can be any historic town within its environment; Dartmouth epitomises every ancient seaport and haven.

I hope something of this essential, archetypal quality of the area, which resonates so strongly for so many people, comes across in this book, and enriches your enjoyment of the Dart between Totnes and the sea. Somehow a journey down a river can be a way of linking oneself to life in an especially deep way, we realise our unity with the past and our

surroundings more readily, so that to travel down a river has become one of the commonest metaphors for life itself. Whenever I am on or near the Dart I feel this more strongly, becoming aware of more each time.

All rivers impinge deeply on our consciousness, and just as for me the Dart is the prototype for them all, so is every other for the people who know and live on it. It has often been noticed that the names given to rivers are curiously obvious and predictable. So many of them just mean 'river' or 'water' (the Avon and Teign), or 'fish' (the Axe and Exe) or in our case, a tree that grows nearby. 'Dart' derives from a Celtic word meaning 'oak', and the tree is still a constant and characteristic sight along the banks. It seems that the very existence of a river is enough for the people who live near it — designation other than merely 'the river' seems hardly necessary, as if it is the only one.

Whatever your native stream may be, the Dart is generally agreed to be special, and is arguably the loveliest river in England. The journey up or down it has been an essential part of any visit to the area for 150 years, its beauties have been celebrated in print many times, and if the language today seems overblown and flowery, the beauty at least has not been exaggerated.

Queen Victoria is said to have been the first to describe the Dart as 'The English Rhine', and the compliment became almost obligatory at a time when taste was formed by continental travel, so that Dartmoor had to be 'Devonia's Alps' and Torquay the 'English Naples'. I have even seen Lynton and Lynmouth referred to as the 'English Switzerland', an unlikely comparison, one would have thought, owing to that country's lack of sea-coast and the very definite presence of just that geographical feature in North Devon! Torbay still sells itself as the 'English Riviera' but in general such titles seem dated and inept.

This little book is written from the viewpoint of someone travelling from Totnes to Dartmouth on one of the pleasure boats — my instinct is still to call them steamers — which run throughout the summer, a journey of about twelve miles taking one and a quarter hours. Clearly it is impossible in a book of this size to cover anything like all that could be said about the tidal Dart, especially by someone to whom it has been a lifelong presence. But I hope it will encourage people going in either direction to get to know the area of the river by walking or driving to the places mentioned, exploring the villages and countryside seen from the water, and sampling some of the delightful riparian hostelries along the way!

The River Dart begins its life high up in one of the bleakest and most remote parts of Dartmoor, in the great northern bog which gives birth to most of Devon's famous rivers. The area has been likened to a sponge that absorbs the rain and then squeezes it out again as streams which, joining together, become the great waterways radiating out over the county bringing the fertility and lushness for which Devon is noted. The Dart's total length is about forty five miles and the whole area of the river is rich in beauty, character and historical interest. By the time it gets to Totnes, the lowest bridging point, the Dart

has reached its final stage in life, as a broad, deep tidal estuary, a major feature in the social and economic life of South Devon for as long as people have lived here.

Camden, the sixteenth century antiquary, described Totnes succinctly as 'a little town hanging from East to West on the side of a hill', and the Devon writer Thomas Westcote, a hundred years later, called it 'this city-like town' with 'pleasant soil, fruitful country and healthful air'. These clear, unadorned images still say something essential about the place, with its red sandstone church tower visible for miles in every direction, fine old buildings, steep streets and grey, valerian-covered walls. Totnes is one of the oldest boroughs in Devon, and has a place in mediaeval legend as the landing site of Brutus the Trojan, founder of the British people. Totnes today is far from being anything like an average small town, having become something of a magnet for all kinds of artistic, educational, spiritual and 'alternative' activities and is enjoyably cosmopolitan. It is full of book shops, good pubs and many subcultures!

However, tempting as it is, we must not dwell on the wonders of Totnes but confine ourselves to the town's relationship to the river (see *The Great Little Totnes Book* by Chips Barber, for a full picture). If you climb to the top of the Norman castle and walk round the battlements you can look down and see exactly why and how the town came to be just where it is: the hill for defence, the river for trade and communications. From here the mediaeval merchants could have watched the ships coming in laden with wine and spices from France, Italy and Portugal; in 1588 you may have seen the two ships fitted out by the people of Totnes and Dartmouth to fight the Armada and in any century up to our own, vessels coming and going with all the trade and produce of a rich agricultural centre. In early centuries Totnes acquired its wealth from tin and cloth, while later on, cider, wool, cloth and timber were all sent out of the port.

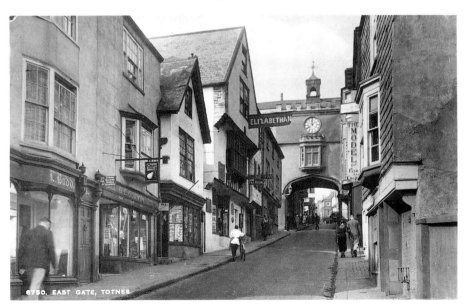

Another good place from which to appreciate the natural setting of Totnes in relation to its river is the southern part of the old town behind the Civic Hall where South Street divides into two levels. The steep hillsides of the long river valley stretch away to the south east, the little town seems to grow inevitably up the slopes.

By the sixteenth century the tin mining on Dartmoor had caused the Dart to silt up badly. The Elizabethan poet Edmund Spenser, inviting the rivers of England to the marriage of Thames and Medway in his *Faerie Queen*, says of the Dart only that it is 'nigh choaked with sands of tinnie mines.' This may be disappointing, but he is better than his contemporary Michael Drayton, who in his long topographical poem *Polyolbion* manages only to say, after a lot of words, that of all Dartmoor's rivers, this is the only one that is named after it's birthplace! The Dart has not done terribly well for poetry.

At the end of the eighteenth century the silting had become so bad that vessels of any size could not get up to Totnes any more, but had to anchor down at Sharpham Point, some way from the town, and the cargoes were transported backwards and forwards by local watermen in fleets of small boats. That the river did not silt up completely, leaving the port high and dry, is thanks to the work of Edward Augustus Seymour, the 11th Duke of Somerset (1775–1855).

From the mid-sixteenth century the Seymours had owned the nearby manor of Berry Pomeroy and the borough of Bridgetown, which had grown up on the opposite side of the river from Totnes during the middle ages. They lived in grand style at Berry Pomeroy Castle until the end of the seventeenth century when they moved to their other seat at Maiden Bradley in Wiltshire, so as to be closer to London and the great world. They never parted with their estates in Devon, however, and the 11th Duke resided at Stover near Newton Abbot. He took a strong proprietorial interest in Totnes and Bridgetown (the latter had ceased to be a separate borough in 1835). He laid out the castle grounds, extended the small island in the river to make the pleasant park now known as Vire Island, embanked the river for a mile on the left hand side and built several streets of attractive, dignified houses and cottages in Bridgetown. His main aim was to save Totnes as a port, and he was instrumental in setting up, in 1834, the River Dart Navigation Commission, with responsibility for the state of the river banks and the dredging of sand down to as far as the confluence of Bow Creek with the Dart. Thirty years later the Dart Harbour Commission was founded to care for the rest of the river. In 1976 both bodies were combined into the Dart Harbour Navigation Authority which has jurisdiction over the whole length of the tidal estuary, from Totnes weir downwards. The work of these organisations

has enabled both Totnes and Dartmouth to survive as ports until today.

The Seymour influence is still apparent in Berry Pomeroy and Bridgetown, the present, 19th, Duke of Somerset being actively concerned with the area, much of which he still owns. Bridgetown itself rarely gets much attention, being usually dismissed as a suburb of Totnes. In fact the older, lower part of Bridgetown, centred around St John's Church, a few shops and the Albert Inn, has a close, village-like identity of its own, is full of good domestic architecture of all periods, and is a most agreeable place to live. If you stand between Bridgetown and Totnes on the graceful bridge built by Charles Fowler in 1828 and look upstream at low tide, you can see clearly the foundations of the earlier mediaeval bridge in direct line with Totnes' main street. From here some steps take you down to a very enjoyable Riverside Walk which skirts the town's industrial estate and follows the riverbank through trees and undergrowth, beneath the railway and on to the weir and the Dartington Hall drive. It is an excellent walk for observing wildlife — not only swans and ducks but sandpipers and the occasional kingfisher can be seen — but by the time we reach the weir it is apparent that, with its low-lying water-meadows and reed banks, we are at an earlier stage in the river's life than the estuary which concerns this book, so we must retrace our steps and just find time to visit Vire Island, on the opposite side of the bridge.

Long known simply as The Island, this was created out of two smaller ones between which a ford crossed the river before ever a bridge was thought of. Renamed Vire Island after the town in Normandy with which Totnes was twinned in 1973, it is a beautifully green, shady place to spend an hour or two watching the river and its life, the people and the ducks and swans.

It is all very peaceful, but be warned: however placid the river may look from here, especially in the summer, it is in reality a dark old god and can be dangerous. Look down from the bridge at low tide and see the violent currents and cross-currents or observe it fast and swollen after heavy rain. The old, much-quoted story is that each year the river demands and takes a life. Most people know a variant of the couplet which I first heard as:

Dart! Dart! Evil Dart!
Ev'ry year thou claim'st a heart!

The people who live along the river, from the remote settlements of Dartmoor down to Dartmouth and Kingswear, take this to be no less than the truth, and accept it as a fact of life. And, indeed, it does seem to be the case that every year somebody, somewhere along the river, is drowned. The older most indigenous locals even seem relieved when it happens, and say that of course it's sad, but at least the river has had its life for one year! In 1980 the life was my father's, and that is what some of them said to me.

Before leaving Totnes, make sure you see the Guildhall, church and Museum, and take in something of the unique atmosphere, mellow but lively, of the old town. However, we cannot linger any more, but must get across to Steamer Quay, on the Bridgetown side, for the trip down river.

Two companies, G.H. Ridalls and Sons ('the Red Cruisers') and Dart Pleasure Craft Ltd ('River Link'), run sailings from here daily from Easter to the end of October, the times varying according to the tide. The vessels of both firms are equipped with bars and the skippers provide an entertaining commentary throughout the journey. They also make the same jokes about each other's fleets.

I cannot remember a time when I wasn't familiar with Steamer Quay and the comings

and goings of the river-boats. During the summer of 1967 I virtually lived there; my mother was running the cafe and I spent my days hanging around, getting to know the steamers and the men who worked them. So much has that time and place become part of my life that I am always vaguely surprised when I go there that it is not just as it was when I was seven. In fact it hasn't changed too much — the dark wooden cafe and little pebble-dash ticket office are still there, though the quay itself has been enlarged, steps have replaced the brown wooden gangplanks which used to be rolled out, and that pile of tyres has appeared. The blue boats of River Link and the red boats of Ridalls have replaced the white 'castle' boats of the River Dart Steamboat Co Ltd which I knew so well (actually, a few of them are the same, heavily disguised with new colour and superstructure). The Steamer Quay of my childhood can still be recognised but, as I write, the future of this whole area is so uncertain that before long it could well look very different.

And so, at last, after a rambling introduction, we set out from the old quayside, as thousands have done every year for over a century, for the famous trip down the River

Dart! For an hour and a quarter we shall be well away from the most pervasive sights and sounds of the late twentieth century, in view of no main roads or motor traffic. Even the minor roads tend to be away from the river, and only occasionally, driving from Totnes to Stoke Gabriel or Cornworthy to Dittisham, will you get a fleeting glimpse of shining water. We shall be passing through deep countryside surrounded by high rounded hills, the light green of the fields and patches of red ploughland standing out in striking contrast to the more ubiquitous dark tone of the trees that line the banks so much of the way. From the journey down the river you will take away an impression, never to be lost, of the endless hillsides, wooded cliffs, stretches of saltmarsh and photogenic boathouses right on the water's edge, seemingly inaccessible from anywhere. We pass the places from which people have gone out to discover 'new worlds' and where they have been inspired for creativity and invention. There are, surprisingly, no stories of tragedy (except the annual one) or mystery associated with the lower Dart, but we sail right past the home of Agatha Christie, a master teller of them. Lovers of natural history will be constantly absorbed in the richness of bird, mammal and plant life, and as well as the literary and historical connections there are unexpected links with films and television. However well you may know the river, there is always something new to discover.

At first we pass, on both sides, a pleasantly untidy jumble of past and present industrial

and commercial activity. In this century, Totnes as a port has meant mainly sand dredging, timber importing and some boat building. Up until the 1930s Thames barges used to call here, bringing cement and taking away the cider which, if the tributes to it in print are anything to go by, was pretty potent stuff! During the Second World War, wooden minesweepers were built here. The little quay on the right where the sand was brought is now deserted. It has been estimated that millions of tons were taken out of the river from the time of the Navigation Commission until 1983 when dredging ceased — the old low sand dredger with its crane was another familiar sight of my childhood. The timber yard of F.J. Reeves Ltd is still busy, however. This has been a major Totnes employer since 1896, when a Russian ship, the *Ekonom*, brought the first cargo of timber. Today most of it comes from Poland and Scandinavia, but over the years German, Dutch, Finnish and Irish ships have been brought up the river by local pilots.

Climbing steeply up the great hillside above the woodyard is Totnes Down Hill, a very narrow road to Ashprington, Bow Bridge and Tuckenhay, affording spectacular views of Totnes, Bridgetown and away

to Dartmoor. Lower down and less steep runs Sharpham Drive, along which an invigorating walk, with the river in view most of the way, can be taken across the hills and fields to Sharpham and Ashprington. At the end of Reeves' yard the trees come right down the hillside to the water's edge, a first brief statement of what is to be the Dart's main theme.

On the other side of the river, past the boatyards and the large triangular turning bay, cut out in the early 1970s to enable bigger timber boats to get away once they had arrived, we pass what is left of the Longmarsh, created in the last century by the embanking activities of the Duke of Somerset, and a much loved recreational area. On maps it is still referred to as a Rifle Range; it was originally used as such by the local militia and again in both world wars. In my boyhood, much of which I spent roaming here, it was a wonderful place; since then it has been raised by several feet and the path has been tidied up. It is no doubt still an enjoyable walk for locals and their dogs, but it can never be what it was.

At the end of the Longmarsh, on the opposite side, the trees give way to a low, flat area with the matchlessly atmospheric name of World's End. This is the site of the old Totnes sewage works, which on hot summer days smelt very much like the end of the world. The retaining wall along here, keeping the river from the salt-marshes, was originally built by French prisoners during the Napoleonic Wars.

On the left hand side, high on the hill, is the ruin of a farm cottage and outbuildings also with an appropriate name 'Windwhistle'. It was last inhabited during the early years of this century, and when the local volunteers were doing their shooting practice on the Longmarsh, a red flag would be flown from here to warn people to keep well away.

Turning again to the right bank, there is a large gap in the wall known locally as the Hole in the Wall. Twenty five years ago that is all it was, but now unless something is done it is going to go on increasing and drastically affect the level of the river.

On the left, just visible among the trees, is an interesting old ruin called Parker's Barn. All that anyone knows about it is the much-repeated story of how, in the days when Totnes was the most corrupt of Rotten Boroughs, a man called Parker was brought here during an election, plied with drink, and locked up until the voting was over. In those days when the franchise was limited and the voting done openly, everybody knew that one man's vote could make all the difference, and Parker was that one man (he must also have been pretty thick to have accepted an invitation to a drinking party in a barn half-way down the river on the day of the election, but let that pass).

The river now begins to twist and turn, first to the right and then the left, in a seductive series of curves and wiggles. (Dammit, I was determined not to fall into the tiresome anthropomorphic mannerisms of so many topographical writers!) Here we look back for our last view of Totnes with its rose-red church tower, if not 'half as old as time', at least a respectable half millennium. The commentators on the boats always say that if you can see the hills of Dartmoor from here it is going to rain, and if you can't see them, it is already raining.

Cormorants are a common sight throughout the journey, either fishing or sitting, wings outstretched, to dry out on the trees. Shelduck are also likely to be around, and Canada geese, relative newcomers to the Dart, nest hereabouts.

Over on the left now is an old low wall. This is Fleet Mill Quay, and lying against it is a rusting iron hulk. This was once one of the River Dart paddle steamers, the first *Kingswear Castle*. Built in 1904, she worked the river until 1924, then served for a while in Dartmouth harbour as an isolation hospital ship. To avoid infection, she was burnt out

and brought here, where she will no doubt remain until she disintegrates into the mud.

The first paddle steamer on the river was *The Dart* of 1837. During the middle years of the century the traffic began to take off, with great rivalry between companies similar to that of the railways. The famous 'castle' ships of the River Dart Steamboat Co Ltd began in 1880 with *Berry Castle*, but for anyone who can remember steam on the Dart, the inevitable picture that comes to mind is of the three vessels that plied up and down for forty years until, in the early 1960s, they literally failed their MOTs (what an ignominious end for such beautiful craft!): *Compton Castle*, *Totnes Castle* and the second *Kingswear Castle*. They have been called the most distinctive paddlers ever to grace an English river, and grace it they certainly did, although some of the more fastidious guide-book writers disliked them for their noise and popularity. To me as a little boy they were magical, and as inseparable from the river as the swans and the banks themselves. *Compton Castle* was the first to be withdrawn, and after many vicissitudes is now at Truro, where I came upon her one wet Sunday morning in February, landlocked and barely recognisable. *Totnes Castle*, on her way to the breakers in Plymouth, elected instead to go down in heavy seas off Burgh Island in Bigbury Bay, but fortunately *Kingswear Castle*, of 1924, last to be built and last to go, survives, beautifully restored by the Paddle Steamer Preservation Society, and can be found, far from home, at work on the Medway, the last British river paddler in the world.

The last man to skipper a paddle steamer on the Dart was Bill Rehberg, a popular figure in Dartmouth, who sadly died just before I was able to talk to him for this book, ending a tradition going back 150 years. He spent forty nine years with the RDSC, and I got to know him when he had Kingswear's motor replacement, the *Cardiff Castle*, which is still here, though different in appearance. Long service seems to have been a tradition amongst the men on the river-boats, but then, what a way to spend one's working life!

The motor boats of both River Link and Ridall's are not without elegance or interest, and both fleets contain veterans who answered the call and went to Dunkirk.

Meanwhile, the old *Kingswear Castle* before us rusts quietly away beside the marsh plants and water birds. Not all of her though, because her namesake inherited her engines. The nature columnist of the *Totnes Times*, who knows these waters well, tells me that at night she comes back to life and heads down river with a jazz band on board and crowds of dancing children, animals and elves. He also states that there are dragons nesting along this part of the river but, although I am all for a little whim, I fear I have not seen them.

Fleet Mill Quay was the landing place for the ships belonging to the Seymours at Berry Pomeroy Castle. Their prizes would be taken from here past Fleet Mill and up the steep packhorse lane to the castle. This lane, a lovely example of a deep, hidden, Devon track, is said to be occasionally haunted by the ghost of a beautiful young girl, but I have been unable to find out any more. There are plenty of spirits at the nearby castle, however, and *The Ghosts of Berry Pomeroy Castle* by Deryck Seymour, will tell you all about them!

On the left now the hillside becomes steeper and the trees denser, and you will notice how they are cut off neatly at the bottom in a perfectly straight line. This is of course the work of the salt water at its highest point, but the skipper will tell you that it is his winter job to go up and down the river in a rowing boat cutting the branches off with shears!

The appearance of these tree-covered hills is an endless delight, but the way to enjoy them is from the river or the opposite bank. I suppose I always knew this, and it was confirmed by the only experience I have had of plunging into them.

A few years ago a friend who had not been in the area long wanted to go for a walk in the vicinity of the river. I designed a pleasant stroll across the hills and along the lanes to Stoke Gabriel, where I fondly planned to have lunch at a pub. However, my companion wanted to remain in view of the river all the way, which I knew was impossible but, being ever-flexible, I did not argue. This meant that after Fleet Mill quay there was no alternative to seeking a path through these very woods, so peaceful-looking from the river, which quickly became completely impenetrable. Unable to go on or back, we had to drop down onto the rocks — fortunately the tide was low, or that wouldn't have been an option — and continue along them until we eventually reached a way out opposite Sharpham boathouse. We arrived in Stoke Gabriel, torn, bedraggled and covered in mud, in time for nothing more than a cup of tea at about four o'clock (this was before all-day opening!), which was not how I had envisaged it at all.

For a while now on the right-hand side we have been passing the Sharpham estate, the largest on the banks of the Dart, stretching for two and three quarter miles. The house, coming into view up on the ridge, is an impressive but rather austere Georgian building begun in 1770, although there was an earlier Sharpham House lower down near the river. It was designed by Sir Robert Taylor and the grounds are said to have been laid out by Capability Brown, but are more likely to be by one of his followers. The house was commissioned by a successful naval officer, Captain Philemon Pownall, who paid for it with the £65,000 he took as his share from a captured Spanish vessel. Unfortunately, the Captain was killed in action ten years after work began (his monument can be seen in nearby Ashprington church), and the house was not completed until 1826. Sharpham has had various owners over the years, including the Bastards, a distinguished Westcountry family, and the Durants, who are remembered in the atmospheric Durant Arms in Ashprington. It is still in private hands and not usually open to visitors, but part of the house is home to the Sharpham North Community, a focus for many of the spiritual, holistic and green activities for which the Totnes area is noted. In front on the terrace are a Henry Moore reclining woman and a 'Persephone' by Barbara Hepworth.

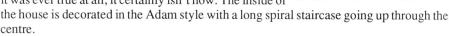

Ignore what they tell you about Sharpham being a 'calendar house' with 365 windows, 52 rooms etc. — if it was ever true at all, it certainly isn't now. The inside of the house is decorated in the Adam style with a long spiral staircase going up through the centre.

Down at the water's edge is the toy-like Sharpham Boathouse, which must be one of the most photographed sights on the river. For a while during the late 1970s this was the home of the Liverpool poet Brian Patten.

Sharpham is a place of meditation, art and music, and it is easy to appreciate why. The wonderful sweep of Sharpham woods, rising to nearly 300 feet, now occupies our whole attention, whether we are watching for birds or just absorbing the sight of these dense curtains of oak and sycamore. It is a beautiful place to pass through at any time, but my most magical experience of it was early one misty September day when I came this way in a boat with some young people who thought they were going to be film stars. They turned out to be wrong, as you will read shortly, but the loveliness of that morning trip on the river must surely have been more than compensation.

As for the bird life: cormorants can usually be seen here, as everywhere else along the route, and their nesting sites, covered in white guano, stand out sharply against the green! A heronry at Sharpham was celebrated for many centuries and, although in recent years they have become scarcer, herons are still found here. If you are fortunate, you will see buzzards and, later in the year, ospreys, hang-gliding dramatically above the wooded cliffs.

The river wends its way around the Sharpham estate, positively loath to leave such a beautiful spot, as it says in a nostalgic little guidebook they used to sell on the steamers, but be that as it may, we must move on, and the next point of interest is the group of three houses immediately on the water-side, up ahead on the left. This is the hamlet of Duncannon, the smallest of the three salmon-fishing settlements on the river. They call it a village, although it is just three houses. The story goes that once during a census — nobody actually knows which one, but it certainly was not the Domesday Book, as is occasionally claimed — a clerical error made the population not thirty but three hundred, enough to officially classify it as a village. All very improbable, and they cap the tale with the information that it is known as the 'village of No Ps', having no parson, no post office, no policeman, no pub, no parking and no public convenience. The trip down the river would just not be the same without hearing that one again, every time!

But whatever they tell you about Duncannon, these old houses with their gardens right against the river, the inevitable backcloth of trees, make a timeless and unforgettable impression, one of those sights that epitomise the essence of the river Dart.

There is another Obelisk Publication which is well worth reading, especially when we get further along the way towards Dartmouth – *Made in Devon* by Chips Barber and David FitzGerald – which is about many of the films, television programmes and advertisements made wholly or partly in this county. One story you will not find in it, however, concerns the steep field which rises up opposite Duncannon, at Ashprington Point. This story is as follows.

One evening in 1988 I was in the Albert Inn, Bridgetown, as usual, when a friend came in and asked me if I would like to be an 'extra' in a TV commercial being made along the River Dart. All I had to do was to be in a certain place at six o'clock the next morning. I was there, as were the half-dozen or so young people mentioned earlier, all fresh and smart and ready for their break into films. Though having no such ambition myself, I looked forward to a day of interest and some extra cash in my pocket. We were brought to the bottom of this field opposite Duncannon in a Landrover, and saw a boat appear, most romantically, out of the mist. We boarded it without question, and moved silently through the water, past the woods of Sharpham, past the mysterious skeleton of the *Kingswear Castle* and towards the salt-marshes. By this time I had picked up the information that we were to be filmed, milling around, at a country fair that was to take place in the field. Why then was the field empty, and we in a boat within sight of Totnes church?

When we landed it all became clear. Yes, we were told, a country fair in that field was to be part of the advertisement, but they weren't ready to film it yet. What we were wanted for today was to work, up to our knees, in black marsh-mud, cutting down reeds and binding them up. Not surprisingly only two of us in the boat chose to stay and do this, which we did far into the evening.

Months later I saw the commercial, which was for a certain petrol. It was all about transformation, appropriately enough for this part of South Devon. Various kinds of vehicle were shown from the point of view of someone inside them, racing along different terrains and changing into something else, demonstrating the versatility of the particular brand of petrol. The shots

that concerned our efforts were of a speedboat on the river. It seems to disappear into a bank of reeds at the water's edge and become a Landrover which climbs the field where the fair is taking place. There is no bank of reeds at the water's edge of Ashprington Point, so this is why we were cutting them down. They were brought here and placed around the ramp onto which the speedboat leapt. The reeds, and we cut an awful lot of them, must have been in camera for at least a second!

Looking ahead now, it is not at all clear which way the river is going to go, to the right or left. Actually, the right fork is Bow Creek, which links the two little rivers of Harbourne and Wash, and the settlements of Tuckenhay and Bow Bridge, to the Dart. But before we go on to explore the pleasures of Bow Creek and its environs, there are a couple of faint literary recollections from this reach of the river that, although the works of both authors are little read nowadays, may be of some interest. Eden Phillpotts (1862–1960) had a long and prolific career as novelist and man of letters, and is remembered in particular for his cycle of eighteen Dartmoor novels. *The Ring Fence* is set not on the moor, but here by the River Dart, featuring Duncannon and Stoke Gabriel as 'Greencannon' and 'Thorpe Michael'. Like most of his work, it is a lively, gentle and loving tale of ordinary Devon people, made especially realistic by his use of common local surnames and recognisable places, and by his masterly rendering of the soft, rich dialect of our 'laukel spaich'.

The works of Eden Phillpotts are worth reading and can still be found, even if only in second-hand book shops. You would be very fortunate indeed, however, to find any of the books that came out under the name of Elliot Plain, though not if you had to pay very much for them! Elliot Plain is a small street in Buckfastleigh, higher up the Dart, and it was the pseudonym of Walter Holdsworth (1881–1947), who was born on a farm just outside the town. He used Westcountry stories and folk material to express his view of life, which was profoundly pessimistic: if anything can go badly it will, and will probably be far worse than anyone could have reasonably predicted. This would be fine, but the problem is that Plain was a terrible writer, and his effects rarely came off. He used the same theme in tale after tale, a favourite being the 'Widecombe Fair' story, that of a group of simple Devon people out for a day's enjoyment, who instead are overtaken by tragedy. This is the structure of the book which concerns us here, *Us River Men*. The title is the best thing about it. The story is of a crowd of Dartmouth men who decide to spend the day at Totnes market, and to travel there and back in a borrowed boat. All goes well until the return journey — they have spent the day in the inns and taverns of Totnes, and have

difficulty handling the boat. Eventually it sinks, just here between Duncannon and Bow Creek. They are all about to drown when a paddle steamer appears round the bend and rescues them, although they never recover from the shock, and the owner of the lost boat dies broken-hearted. It is all very silly, and badly written as well, but Elliot Plain was genuinely popular in his day.

If we imagine for a minute that we are not on the steamer — sorry, motor vessel — but in our own boat, and able to go where we fancy, we can, as many people do, not follow the course of the river just yet, but make a diversion to the right into Bow Creek. The water flows peacefully for a couple of miles between typical Dartside scenery until it narrows and divides into the Wash on the left and the Harbourne ahead. Here is the interesting and attractive little village of Tuckenhay, which has an industrial history unusual in a place so small. The name reveals that it has always been a place of mills, hay meaning a field and 'tucking' being the local word for fulling. In the nineteenth century there were a corn and two paper mills, numerous lime kilns can be found in the area and large quantities of stone used to be taken away from the extensive quays here to be used for road making in London and elsewhere. The last paper mill worked until the 1970s, and the fine handmade paper was used for English and American banknotes. It is also usually stated that Tuckenhay had gas lighting in

1806, the year that London first got it so, for anyone interested in the industrial past — still not the first thing that many people associate with a small Devon village — the place will provide much to absorb.

A little way along the Harbourne is the local hostelry, the Maltsters Arms, long noted for its food and water-side setting. Lots of people like to come by boat to this pleasant old pub, but if you do, make sure you know the tide timetable, as more than one party has been spoiled by a sea of mud between the meal and the return journey! In 1989 the pub was discovered and purchased by the ebullient TV chef Keith Floyd, who has again made it one of the most popular eating places in the area. And not much more than a mile along the road, if that, we come to another old inn famous for its food and the beauty of its position, the Waterman's Arms at Bow Bridge, and a highly atmospheric place it is. From here the road climbs steeply back to Totnes, or it is barely a five-minute walk to the almost-too-pretty-to-be-true village of Ashprington, whose enjoyable pub has already been mentioned. The area of Bow Creek is truly one of many delights.

Dragging ourselves away, however, and returning down the creek to the river, we enter Long Stream. The Dart is now a wide estuary, similar to but less encroached upon than those of the Teign and Exe, and more interestingly broken up by inlets and curves. Long Stream is known as 'the Lake of the Dart' – it certainly does resemble one, there being no obvious way out at either end. Though the trees are still ever present, the right bank in particular reveals typical Devon countryside of small variegated fields and hedges, and along this side there are what were once the experimental cider orchards of 'Whiteways'. Up on the left we shall soon be within sight of the large riverside village of Stoke Gabriel. This has always been a place of fishing and of orchards, though many of the latter now have bungalows in them, and is a place of great beauty and interest. In this century Stoke

Gabriel has grown considerably by becoming a popular retirement village, and there is a decidedly up-market feel to many of its attractive and varied houses, yet it remains a real community. My impression from the pubs is that indigenous locals, with names that have been common here for centuries, and new residents co-exist in this gentle environment without too many difficulties. Stoke Gabriel still feels like a village, even if, as I write, the housing and industrial estates of Paignton seem to come ever closer across the red and green hills...

The mellow little church of St Gabriel is worth a visit, with its peaceful churchyard looking out over the water. The churchyard is dominated by a magnificent yew tree, said to be over a thousand years old and one of the largest in England. Certainly it has a wonderful presence, and one person I brought here was almost compelled to worship at it. Just outside the churchyard is my favourite pub in Stoke Gabriel, the Church House Inn, old and comfortable yet smart, which has on display in the bar a mummified pussy-cat, 'Thea', found in the wall of a nearby building!

The Old Yew Tree, Stoke Gabriel (known to be over 1000 years old)

A little along the road to Totnes is Rowe's Farm, which was the birthplace of one of the greatest railway engineers, George Jackson Churchward (1857–1933). The Churchwards were farming in Stoke Gabriel several centuries ago, and the name is still found here. Young George went to Totnes Grammar School, then at the age of sixteen became an apprentice on the Great Western Railway at Newton Abbot engine sheds. In 1902 he succeeded William Dean as Locomotive Superintendent of the GWR, a very powerful and respected position on the railways at that time. Churchward was one of the most innovative locomotive designers, his achievements including the Saint and Star express engines, and later engineers were greatly influenced by his ideas. He always retained a strong Devon accent, and his down-to-earth manner endeared him to his workmen. He was killed tragically whilst crossing the line at Swindon, shortly after his retirement.

Churchward's effect on railway engine design was far-reaching, and it is good to know that one of his engines, albeit a modest tank locomotive, No. 4555, can be seen at work on the Torbay and Dartmouth Steam Railway, which we meet up with a little further on, with his house at Maypool, now a youth hostel, standing high above both railway and river.

Stoke Gabriel has always been the centre of the Dart salmon-fishing industry. There are currently eighteen boats licensed to fish on the estuary, and traditionally the right to a licence was passed down from father to son. The season lasts from the middle of March to the middle of August, allowing the fishermen to work every day during daylight hours except for Saturdays and Sundays. Most of the men today have to have other jobs, as the costs of boats, licences and equipment continue to rise, but they still go out, and the family traditions remain. Each boat has a crew of four, and they can be seen working from the various beaches along the river. What happens is this: one man stands at the water's edge

holding an end of the long seine net, and the boat, with the other end, is rowed out in an arc around the area where the fish have been sighted. The net is then hauled in to the beach, hopefully containing at least one Dart salmon! It is expensive, hard and sometimes dangerous work, but the Dart is still one of the best rivers in the South West for salmon, and certainly there is great satisfaction in having a meal of freshly caught fish in one of the riverside pubs (not that one can afford to do it every day). Poaching, naturally, goes on, and I have heard some fine tales about it, but though it may sound like a romantic activity it is not advisable.

Moving on now from Stoke Gabriel, with its narrow streets and air of quiet gentility, we pass on the left the estate of Sandridge Park. The name derives from that of the family who held it from the Bishop of Exeter in the time of Henry II. Sandridge also has associations with such distinguished local families as the Pomeroys and Gilberts. The present Italianate mansion was built in 1802 by John Nash, who designed Regent St in London.

Nearby is Sandridge Barton, the estate farmhouse, which was the birthplace, in 1550, of John Davis, one of the greatest of the Elizabethan sea-dogs, and the one who was least a buccaneer and most a genuinely scientific explorer. Davis emerged from obscurity at the age of twenty eight, having thoroughly learned the seamanship which would take him to the ends of the earth, but, until his last voyage, he always came back to this quiet reach of the Dart, and his wife and most of his friends were from the villages and towns around the estuary. He comes across, in that age of extremes, as a gentle, humane, intellectual and civilised man who was liked and respected equally by the hardened seamen with whom he sailed, the merchants and courtiers who sponsored his voyages, and the native Americans he encountered and with whom he traded. His life's work centred around the search for a North West Passage, that supposed sea-route between North America and the Arctic circle which would enable the English to reach the riches of India and China without incessant confrontations with the Spanish in the South Atlantic. He failed to find it, for the very good reason that there wasn't one to find, but he went further than anyone else, and the homely names he gave to the places he discovered, such as Totnes Roads and Gilbert Sound, are still on the map. He is himself remembered by the Davis Straits, between Labrador and Greenland.

Davis's first expedition, with the two small ships *Sunshine* and *Moonshine*, which left Dartmouth in 1585, is part of the history of world exploration. He was back in those cold waters in the two following years, but in 1583 there were other things to think about than the discovery of trade routes, and he served during the fight against the Armada as pilot to the Lord High Admiral's flagship. In 1592 he was down at the other end of the world, exploring the Straits of Magellan, and it is on this journey that he is credited with noticing the islands which became known as the Falklands, though the general view today is that they were not what he saw, so he can probably be let off that one! In any case, the voyage was hard and trouble-ridden, and he got back to Sandridge exhausted, only to find that his wife had left him.

Davis wrote the first English treatise on navigation, *The Seaman's Secrets*, which was for a long time the standard work, and *The World's Hydrographical Description*, an early and rare study of water in all its manifestations. He also helped to construct the first globes in this country, and his invention of the back-staff for fixing latitudes led directly to the development of the sextant. In 1601 he set out from Dartmouth with what was in effect the first voyage of the East India Company which was to become the basis of the whole British-in-India story, and the world's greatest empire. Whatever we think today of the arrogance with which the European nations went out and took over the rest of the world,

the vision, courage and determination shown by these early adventurers is worthy of respect, and certainly John Davis was one of whom nothing bad seems ever to have been said. He was killed by Japanese pirates in 1605 off the Malayan coast, ironically enough, as he was offering them hospitality at the time.

Over on the right we can see, above the creek inlet, the church and the higher part of Dittisham, the last village on the Dart, but there are a few more things to look at before we talk about Dittisham.

The river now turns right into Broad Stream, which at its widest is a mile across. On the left is the estate of Waddeton Court, the boathouse of which sits dramatically on the water's edge beneath the trees. Waddeton was another Mediaeval estate, the present house being an early nineteenth century 'Elizabethan' style mansion.

If you would like to explore the countryside along this part of the river more thoroughly on foot, there is yet another Obelisk Publication exactly suited to your needs! In *Walking "with a Tired Terrier" in and Around Torbay*, the Paignton artist, writer and naturalist Brian Carter describes some gentle but atmospheric strolls about the area he knows so well, including some riverside walks in the vicinity of Stoke Gabriel, Galmpton and Greenway.

Near Waddeton, concrete ramps and other remains of the Second World War remind us that a large part of the South Devon coast, including the Dart estuary, was used as a preparation and training area by the American forces before the invasion of Normandy, and various other mementos of that time can be seen between here and Dartmouth.

On the far left of Broad Stream is Galmpton Creek, at the end of which we will find the large village of Galmpton, part of the parish of Churston Ferrers, almost in the great urban sprawl of Torbay. Galmpton has long been a local centre of industry, especially boat building, and the famous red-sailed wooden trawlers of Brixham were built here in the nineteenth and early twentieth centuries, though it is no longer the hive of activity it was. We stick closely to the right bank however and, from the river, Galmpton is no more than a distant shoreline of black sheds.

We now approach the lovely village of Dittisham, pronounced 'Ditsam', once renowned for its damsons and plums, which covered the surrounding hillsides and no doubt

Dittisham. River Dart.

contributed to the romantic comparisons between the Dart and the Rhine. In the early years of this century, Dittisham was barely more than one long narrow street, climbing up from the riverside to the church, high on the hill, and you could buy plums from the door of every cottage. Now the orchards have nearly all gone, and the fields are full of expensive houses. Dittisham is certainly home to some wealthy and famous people, the Dimblebys being the best known. I have been told that there are now no more than three born-and-bred locals living here, but I have felt nothing of the unreal atmosphere that you often get in places so taken over by retirement and holiday homes, and some fishing still goes on. As well as its plums, Dittisham was known for another traditional gastronomic delight, which apparently you can still find here — cockles and cream. This consists of freshly picked cockles from the river, with rich Devonshire clotted cream — and nothing else! Along with the salmon, I suppose this must be the ultimate taste of the River Dart.

The Ferry Boat Inn, down on the quay, is a fine old pub, and is associated for many people with the songs and stories of Bill 'Pop' Hingston. In the folk clubs and singing pubs of South Devon you will hear Pop spoken of with love and reverence. He was a real village musician of the traditional kind, with a wealth of songs and tunes from his youth or picked up over a long life.

Another Dittisham character who will be remembered in the Ferry Boat by anyone who has been around for more than thirty years, is Sammy Coombes, who is spoken of with respect and even awe. Sammy Coombes was born with severe physical handicaps, one hand apparently looking 'like a donkey's foot', the other having only one, bent, finger and a thumb. He had one leg so short that he needed a boot fifteen inches high, and his mouth

was twisted with a harelip. Such deformities, especially in a small, remote village in the early part of the century, could have driven a weaker man to lifelong misanthropy or even suicide, but Sammy had a long, fulfilling life. He worked on the river, and was better than anyone else, his skill with boat and knowledge of navigation and fishing making his fame spread naturally throughout the country, and even round the world. He swam 'like a fish' and was so well-read that there was little he couldn't talk about. He too had his song, which he would sing in the pub on Saturday nights: the good old Chaucerian tale of the man who brings home a crab or lobster and leaves it in the chamberpot, but forgets to tell his wife, who discovers it, painfully, the next morning. His choice of such a bawdy, life-loving song says a lot about the spirit of the man, as does the time when Pop Hingston was talking about the handicapped beggars he had seen in India during the War. Said Sammy, 'I bet you never seen an uglier bastard than me in all your life!'

Dittisham has one other musical association, as the birthplace, in 1579, of the Rev. Francis Rous, author of the much-loved hymn based on Psalm 23, *The Lord is My Shepherd*. Coming from here, one reflects, it is easy to see how he could have evoked so well the 'pastures green' and 'quiet waters.'

Opposite Dittisham and linked by ferry is the highly photogenic Greenway Quay, the cottage there being over 400 years old. The river now narrows and deepens, and the trees on both sides rise up beautifully to hundreds of feet. On the left we pass the Greenway estate, appropriately named for the way the dense woods are reflected in the water giving it a greenish tinge. The present Greenway House is Georgian, but in an earlier building on this site were born three sons of a most remarkable woman, all of whom achieved fame and distinction, and one of whom has a place in English and even world history.

Katherine Champernowne came from an old Devon family associated with both Modbury and Dartington. She first married Otho Gilbert, whose family owned nearby Compton Castle, but who himself lived here at Greenway, where were born John, Humphrey and Adrian Gilbert. After Otho's death, Katherine married Walter Raleigh of Hayes Barton in East Devon, becoming the mother of the greatest Devonian of all in that age when this county produced so many great men, Sir Walter Raleigh, England's most versatile Renaissance genius.

Katherine's eldest son, Sir John, became vice-admiral for Devon, and was responsible for local defences during the Armada crisis. He also presented to Queen Elizabeth what was probably the first parakeet in England, though what she thought of it is unrecorded. Adrian lived at Sandridge and was heavily involved in silver mining in North Devon. He practised astrology and was an associate in the voyages of his neighbour John Davis and other explorers. But in Sir Humphrey Gilbert, born in 1537, we have a personality only less talented and complex than his younger half-brother, Raleigh. 'A high attempting spirit, a skillful mathematician and hydrographer, though not equally favoured by fortune', is how the Devon writer Thomas Risdon described him. He was brilliant, courageous and generous, but could be cruel, and he seemed to lack the ability to inspire confidence in many who were led by him. He is best remembered as the founder of Britain's oldest colony, and for the splendid way he went down with his ship.

His mother's aunt was Kate Ashley, old nurse and confidante to the Princess Elizabeth, and the eighteen-year-old Humphrey was introduced to her household before she became queen. He spent several years soldiering in France and Ireland, where he became known for his brutality — the path to his tent was lined with Irish heads on stakes. In 1570 he entered Parliament for Plymouth, alongside John Hawkins, and published *Queen Elizabeth's Academic*, proposing an elitist but rounded system of education for the sons of the nobility, making them 'philosophers, soldiers and courtiers'. It also seems to have been his idea to have a copy of every book published placed in a central collection, so next time you are in the British Library, spare him a thought. In 1572 he led thousands of volunteers against the Spanish in the Low Countries, but through disunity they achieved nothing remarkable.

Like Davis, Gilbert became obsessed with the discovery of a Northern route to the East, and his great desire was to go and search for it himself, but Queen Elizabeth was reluctant to let him go. Finally in 1578 he was given royal authority to seek out and occupy any lands not already claimed by a Christian king. He left Dartmouth on September 26th with a fleet of twelve ships, one of them commanded by young Walter Raleigh, but the expedition was dogged by bad weather and again by a total lack of unity, with everybody going their own way, getting lost, chasing Spanish vessels then turning for home without saying anything. Gilbert was ruined by the venture, but his spirit was undaunted. He sailed again in 1583, and on August 5th formally laid claim to Newfoundland for the English crown, making it the first colony of what would become the British Empire. On the way back they ran into heavy storms, and Sir Humphrey was last seen on September 9th, sitting calmly on deck with a book in his hand, shouting encouragement to his men and pointing out to them that they were as close to heaven by sea as by land. It is most inspiring to read about, and it is perfectly true that we are as near to heaven in one place as another, but I wonder if, had we been there, we might not have found it rather tiresomely theatrical? Indeed, I cannot help seeing something decidedly 'camp' about it, but that is by the way. Thus perished Sir Humphrey Gilbert of Greenway, whose descendants still live at Compton Castle, just behind Torbay.

The centuries pass, and the old house where Katherine Gilbert's sons were born is replaced by a pleasant Georgian mansion, which in time becomes the home of another very remarkable woman, the best-selling author, Agatha Christie. She was born Agatha Miller in the fashionable resort of Torquay in 1890, and grew up in the town in modest gentility. In 1912 she met a young Army officer, Archie Christie, who later served in the Royal Flying Corps. They were married on Christmas Eve, 1914. During the First World War Agatha served as a nursing assistant and later worked in a dispensary, where she learnt all about poisons. Her daughter Rosalind was born in 1919, and Agatha's first detective novel, *The Mysterious Affair at Styles*, appeared in 1920, after which her career never looked back. During the late 1920s she suffered a nervous breakdown when her marriage came to an end, but the books continued to come out, never less than one each year. She bought Greenway House, in 1938, for £6,000, with her second husband the

archaeologist Sir Max Mallowan, as a summer residence, but for the rest of her life regarded it as her main home. She died in 1976, not at Greenway but at her other home in Oxfordshire.

Her early works are particularly evocative of middle and upper class life in the twenties, set in timelessly peaceful villages and country houses filled with retired colonels, vicars, lively old ladies of independent means, well-meaning but idiotic young men and bright, clever young women who say things like 'It's too frightfully thrilling!' They accept unquestioningly the prejudices of the time, but of course in a Christie novel the convolutions of the plot are all that matters, characters and places only being important in relation to it, and descriptions are kept to a minimum. However, although the reader, concerned only with what happens next, may not necessarily notice it, certain places meant a lot to her, and she often had specific locations in mind, especially the Torquay home of her childhood and early womanhood. The last book published in her lifetime, *Postern of Fate*, a gentle story of a crime long past, seems to have been written largely for the sake of being set there. The River Dart is the setting for two excellent novels of the 1950s. *Dead Man's Folly*, an Hercule Poirot adventure, actually takes place at Greenway, featuring the house, boathouse, quay and the nearby Youth Hostel. At one point, Police Inspector Bland takes a trip up the river, but he only goes as far as Dittisham, known in the story as Gitcham. *Ordeal by Innocence* opens with one of the main characters summoning the ferry from Greenway Quay, crossing to Dittisham and going to a large house Christie invented called Sunny Point, previously known as Viper Point. There is a Viper's Quay actually opposite Greenway, but it is clear from the book that the house is meant to be not here but the other side of Dittisham where the river seems to curve round on itself, at Higher or Lower Gurrow Point. The novel has been filmed, and you can read all about it in *Made in Devon*, which indeed you will need near you for the rest of the journey. There is also a Christie short story, *The Regatta Mystery*, which takes place during Dartmouth's most prestigious annual event .

Greenway is now owned by her daughter, Mrs Rosalind Hicks.

Moving on, we pass, in the middle of the river, the Anchor Stone. Legend persists in making Sir Walter Raleigh come here to smoke his pipe, if not the first pipe he smoked in England. While there is no way of proving that he didn't, the truth is that in his crowded, tumultuous life, he would have had little time for hanging around at Greenway, even though he undoubtedly knew it. The romantic image of Raleigh, the Gilberts and John Davis all growing up together and learning their seafaring skills on the Dart is a misleading one, deriving from the work of the nineteenth century historian James Anthony Froude, himself born in 1818 at Dartington. Froude had a brilliant prose-style, but was a little too partisan to be an accurate historian, especially when it came to his beloved Elizabethans. Raleigh's home was in East Devon, and he was a lot younger than his half-brothers but in the end, the folklore is correct in recognising his links with the place, and if you want to imagine him sitting here on a rock in the middle of the river smoking in the cool of the evening, there were at least a couple of times in his life when he might have done so.

The other story that is always told of the Anchor Stone is that the men of Dittisham used to bring their nagging wives out here and leave them to cool off. While I am with my feminist friends in not finding this particularly hilarious, it is the case that in the sixteenth and seventeenth centuries it was actually on the statute books that every parish should have a ducking stool or similar place of punishment for troublesome characters, and clearly nature had provided Dittisham with an ideal spot for offenders to reflect on their crimes.

Next on the left we come to Maypool, with its Youth Hostel, once Churchward's house, high on the hill. The dark pine trees, standing out against the lighter green of the oaks, are home to a heronry and, although several of them came down in the January storms of 1990, herons still nest here. This is the place where the steam railway from Paignton meets the river, and runs parallel to us from here into Kingswear. The first proposal for a railway into Dartmouth was lodged in 1852, but the Dartmouth and Torbay Railway Act didn't get through parliament until 1857. Brunel was the engineer, and the first sod was cut on January 21, 1858. At that time there were many schemes and ideas for railways into the South Hams (traditionally that part of South Devon between the Dart and the Plym — the present South Hams local authority covers a larger area), and bridges crossing the Dart were suggested in various places. Fortunately perhaps, the railway never did cross the Dart and, apart from the South Brent to Kingsbridge branch, never went south of the main line from Totnes to Plymouth, or maybe today the whole of South Devon might be one big extension of Torbay! Dartmouth was given a station, though, complete with booking office and waiting rooms — everything in fact except a railway line and trains.

Old Mill Creek, River Dart

For over a century it was unique as the only one without them, the passengers being taken across to Kingswear by ferry, and one steam ferry in particular, *The Mew*, working from 1908 to 1955, was perhaps the best loved vessel ever known in Dartmouth harbour.

The railway runs along through the dense forest of Long Wood, the line of the cutting just noticeable about a third of the way up. Long Wood consists of dwarf oaks, planted originally for the charcoal industry, and is owned by the National Trust. The high, tree-covered right bank, from Dittisham to Old Mill Creek, is now owned by the descendants of Sir Walter Raleigh, which makes no difference at all to the credibility of the Anchor Stone story. Somewhere behind here is the highest point along the whole river, Fire Beacon over 500 ft, a signalling place during the days of the Armada. Not far away is an Iron Age settlement at Capton, which is well worth a visit.

The wooded banks on both sides feel as if they go on for ever, and one can easily fancy oneself on some exotic tropical river like the Amazon. In fact, you can read in *Made in Devon* of how, during the filming of the popular serial *The Onedin Line*, they tried to make the Dart into just that river, and with what results. Looking to the right, we pass Kilngate Farm, by the water's edge, where tradition has it that the Pilgrim Fathers held a prayer meeting before what they thought would be their last farewell to England, when they sailed from Dartmouth in the *Mayflower* and *Speedwell* in the summer of 1620. Dartmouth

25

itself was an unscheduled stop, and it must have been a real anti-climax for them when they had to stop again and put into Plymouth, from where they finally set out on September 6th.

On the left we approach the famous shipyard of Philip and Sons at Noss. Founded by a Scotsman, George Philip, in 1858, the firm was for a long time Dartmouth's biggest employer. For over a hundred years a vast range of wooden and steel vessels was built here, from river steamers to Naval and commercial ships of all kinds. Latterly the yard was known for building the Trinity House light-ships, found all around the British and Irish coasts. Chay Blythe's yacht *British Steel* also came from here. The company was sold in 1965 and shipbuilding came to an end in Dartmouth after many centuries, but repair and maintenance work still goes on.

Past the shipyard on the right the river widens for the last time into Old Mill Creek, where you can find a folk-like castle in the woods and the maintenance works for the river-boats. Another paddle steamer lies here: the *Dartmouth Castle* of 1907 plied the river until the outbreak of the Second World War, and was replaced in 1948 by the motor vessel of the same name, which now works for 'River Link'. Whilst back on this subject, *The Dartmothian*, belonging to the Ridall's fleet, formerly the *Seymour Castle*, is particularly indigenous to the river, having been built at Noss in 1938, using oak cut from the banks of Old Mill Creek. The river now begins, as we approach the end of our journey, to be filled up with past and present shipping. The wreck of a wooden Irish ship, the *Invermore*, rests here, near some concrete naval pontoons dating from the Second World War.

Up on the hill above the creek, no doubt affording magnificent views of the harbour, is probably the least attractive building along the river: the Britannia Royal Naval College, where generations of British naval officers have received their training. It was begun in 1902 and finished three years later, to replace two huge wooden hulks, the *Britannia* and the *Hindustan*, which previously housed the cadets, in appalling but no doubt character-building conditions, in the middle of the river. The foundation stone was laid by King Edward VII, and the College has always been closely linked with royalty — enthusiasts for 'Britain's favourite soap-opera' will doubtless know that it was here that the Queen first met her future husband. Every male member of the Royal Family has done his training here, including Princes Charles, Andrew and Edward. But Prince Charles's connection with the Dart is even deeper than this – as Duke of Cornwall he actually owns the riverbed. Below the College the higher car ferry, a diesel-electric paddle-ferry built in 1959, follows wire cables across the river.

The Naval College, Dartmouth.

And so we come into the ancient port of Dartmouth, and all its associations with English and world history. So many pens have overflowed with rapturous descriptions of the beauty of Dartmouth, Kingswear and the harbour entrance that I will not even attempt another one, except to say that it is all true, whatever you think of some of the prose that has been written about it. The loveliness of Dartmouth is of the sort which one can never tire, and I am unashamedly romantic in my enjoyment of the place. Whenever I come here, but especially when I have come down the river, I step into the town with a heightened sense of anticipation and openness. For what, exactly? I am perfectly aware that it is actually a very ordinary little town with all the usual small-town stuff, and its social snobbery is quite blatant, but this does not in any way dampen my feeling of romance and excitement. And the magic works at any time of year and in any conditions. I came down one dull afternoon almost at the end of the season, late in October, and walked through the streets just as a huge downpour was about to drench the area, then sought shelter and refreshment in a conveniently open pub. Nothing much else happened, but the sense of exhilaration and pleasure that being in Dartmouth gave me was unforgettable.

It is impossible here to give anything but the most general overview of Dartmouth's

riches. Explore the feel of the town by walking along the river-front, up and down its steep streets and narrow passages, then sit in the little park next to the boat-float, by the ornate Edwardian bandstand, on which I have played in many a brass band concert, letting the atmosphere sink into you! More specifically, pay a visit to the Museum in the Butterwalk, the church of St Saviours, and Bayard's Cove, which has a miniature castle at one end and which you will instantly recognise from *The Onedin Line*. Then make your way out to Dartmouth Castle and St Petrox Church at the harbour mouth, for a deeper appreciation of the siting and significance of Dartmouth as a port and haven.

The town developed late in comparison with Totnes and other places in the area, but by the Norman conquest there were several small settlements near the river mouth, the seeds for later growth. In 1147 the entire second European Crusade assembled in this magnificent deepwater harbour, and from then on Dartmouth evolved into a major port. The men of the town soon gained a reputation for bold seamanship, piracy and aggression, and many were the skirmishes with the French and the men of other English ports. A long feud existed with Fowey in Cornwall, and it could be that the famous chain, known as Jawbones, which for centuries was stretched across the harbour entrance, was stolen from there.

The most notable of Dartmouth's buccaneer-merchants was John Hawley, who was mayor fourteen times between 1370 and 1408, and is generally credited with being the model for Chaucer's Shipman in the *Canterbury Tales*, though there were many such as he. Hawley was responsible for the first fortifications at the harbour mouth of which a tower and some curtain wall can still be seen. The present castle dates from 1488 and was the first in the country to be designed specifically for artillery. Jawbones was stretched from here to a point called Gomerock on the opposite bank, and was used up to the time of the Civil War, the last twenty feet surviving into the eighteenth century. The vicinity of Dartmouth Castle has continued to be used defensively and fortified up until the Second World War, but Kingswear Castle, built in 1491, was too exposed to be of much value, and in the nineteenth century was converted into a private residence. Until recently it was the summer home of Sir Frederick Bennet, long-serving MP for Torbay.

Back on the Dartmouth side, next to the castle, is the church of St Petrox, dedicated to the most popular of the Westcountry's Celtic missionaries, who may himself have established a chapel here during the sixth century. In the Middle Ages a cell of monks

29

Dartmouth and Kingswear Castles.

maintained a light to guide sailors into the harbour. The present church was built in 1641.

It would need a book in itself to adequately cover the history of Dartmouth, which has more links with our maritime past than anywhere except Plymouth, which overtook it in the sixteenth century. The port is quieter now, but vessels from many countries can be seen in the harbour, and a small crab and fishing fleet still operates, though the emphasis is more on leisure and recreation.

The village of Kingswear is possibly older than Dartmouth, but is almost entirely residential, and perhaps best enjoyed from the opposite bank unless you have a reason for going there. Many years ago I took an enjoyable walk along a road leading through the woods to a point just beyond the castle, and ended up in a steer field with a beach and a cowshed that resembled a miniature fortress. I have heard that both W.S. Gilbert and Sir Arthur Sullivan used to stay in Kingswear, and would argue loudly in the quiet street about the words not fitting the music and the music not fitting the words but, if this is true, no biographer I have consulted deems it worthy of mention.

Above and beyond Dartmouth castle and St Petrox, where the harbour meets the sea is a fitting place to end our journey along the River Dart. I have spent hours here wandering

around the cliff paths and the little coves, or sitting and looking down at the river mouth with its green, tufted cliffs, rocky outcrops and the pale blue of sea and sky. It is all oddly reminiscent of Chinese or Japanese paintings having the same effortless, eternal quality. And when you finally decide to move on you can go from Dartmouth into the deep South Hams with its dramatic coastline and rich countryside, or take the steam train from Kingswear to the bright lights of Torbay. Or you can take the boat back up the river to Totnes.

Although it is natural for me to think of and describe the journey down river, I would agree with those who say that the cumulative effect of the trip in the opposite direction is even more beautiful — the hypnotic green hills on both sides up to Dittisham, the broad, lake-like expanse of Long Stream opening out, only to narrow into the loveliness of Sharpham woods, providing a totally satisfying culmination of all that has gone before, then the natural site of Totnes, when it appears, seems even more perfect and inevitable.

The River Dart from Totnes to Dartmouth, with all its landscapes, its sights and smells, its swans and cormorants and its memories of steamboats, even the patter of the commentators, those dreadful jokes and wild inaccuracies which have nevertheless become part of the scene and therefore to some extent 'true', has haunted my life for as long as I can remember, and been a constant fixture in my consciousness. Writing this short book has only deepened and increased my feeling of connection with it all. I hope that reading it has  enhanced your enjoyment and appreciation of the river, whether you are travelling on it for the first or the hundredth time, and that your journey on the Dart is made a more memorable and satisfying experience.

TELEVISION PROGRAMMES, ADVERTS AND FILMS ALL ...
MADE IN DEVON, Chips Barber and David FitzGerald
Devon has been used extensively for the making of many films, adverts and television programmes. *Made in Devon* is a comprehensive and entertaining guide to a vast number of film productions made all over the county. It is packed with amazing behind-the-scenes stories and reveals the tricks of how film makers have turned Devon into the Mediterranean, Tropical Rain Forest, Monte Carlo, Distant Planets, Scotland, West Indian islands, California and many other places. When you read this book you will be amazed at how many famous and well known film stars have visited Devon. This makes *Made in Devon* an 'absolute must' for any film buff or telly addict.

THE TOTNES COLLECTION, Bill Bennett
Bill Bennett, former Mayor of Totnes, is one of them most popular and best known authorities on the town and its history and has served Totnes in many capacities throughout the years. In this book he has drawn on the collection of photographs belonging to the Totnes Museum Society and selected a wide range of pictures to show celebrations, coronations, sporting teams, local characters and some unusual street scenes from the past.

THE GREAT LITTLE TOTNES BOOK, Chips Barber with Bill Bennett
The Great Little Totnes Book is a wonderful souvenir for both the visitor to Totnes and the interested local. Beautifully illustrated, it is written in a light-hearted fashion by Chips Barber, with expert guidance from Bill Bennett, former Mayor of Totnes and Custodian of Totnes Museum. This informative and entertaining little book features the town's legends, historical events, famous visitors, important buildings, hotels and pubs, shops and much more.

WALKING 'WITH A TIRED TERRIER' IN AND AROUND TORBAY, Brian Carter
In the company of his trusty Jack Russell terrier Jamie, Brian explores a patch of countryside he has known and loved all his life – the towns, hills, valleys and coastline around Torbay – and entertainingly relates his experiences and observations, creating a perfect guide for anyone wishing to enjoy a short stroll in this area – even if they don't have their own little terrier to tire out!

THE GHOSTS OF BERRY POMEROY CASTLE, Deryck Seymour
Berry Pomeroy Castle! To some people it is 'just an interesting old ruin', to some it is a place of great terror and they swear never to go near it again, and to others it is a place of great fascination, reaching out to their subconscious, willing them to research its darkest secrets. Deryck Seymour falls into the last category! His fascination with Berry Pomeroy dates back to his childhood and, knowing that he is a great authority on the subject, many people have told him of their experiences. He has now compiled and categorised these experiences into this fascinating little book – no wonder it is regarded as "The Most Haunted Castle in Britain".

BURGH ISLAND AND BIGBURY BAY, Chips Barber and Judy Chard
This little book is packed with stories from this area and is the perfect informative souvenir of any visit, however brief. Ghost stories, disasters, dark deeds, famous visitors, smuggling, violent vicars, wildlife, past industries and many more tales from Burgh Island and the villages along the Bigbury Bay shoreline are included for your pleasure. You'll be surprised just how much this little book contains.